HOW TO CREATE A SUCCESSFUL REMOTE WORK CULTURE

A Guide to Using the PPAS Maturity Model®

Ute Franzen-Waschke

the three
tomatoes
Book Publishing

Published April 2021
Printed in North America and Europe

ISBN: 978-1-7364949-2-9

For information address:
The Three Tomatoes Book Publishing
6 Soundview Rd.
Glen Cove, NY 11542
www.thethreetomatoespublishing.com

Illustrations: Malin Rena Tesch and Natalie Waschke

Cover design: Malin Rena Tesch and Susan Herbst

Book interior: Susan Herbst

Dedication

This book is dedicated to my husband Joachim Waschke, who encouraged me to "sit down and do it" in many conversations on our balcony during the COVID-19 summer of 2020 in Rochester, MI, USA.

Foreword

As an adviser and coach for organizations in need of change it has always been an exciting moment when I first step through the physical or virtual door of a new client. Actually, this first moment has always been a virtual encounter as the first contact with the client is always by telephone or email. Only later we would have met in other spaces: at their corporate headquarters' offices, a café, an airline lounge or in an online video call.

Following a due diligence process, I would have researched the new client online and maybe tried to reach out to colleagues who had been working with the same organization in order to gain some first-hand information. In the moment when the first substantial conversation with the client happened, I had already formed my initial set of assumptions about their corporate culture. I used to joke that most organizations fall into one of two categories (obviously with space in between the two extremes): either this company feels like a torture chamber in which people dread to enter the doors in the morning and happily leave after a hard-working day – or it is a great place to work where the mantra *Thank God, it's Monday* is what employees identify with every day.

Corporate culture does not fall from heaven – it is building up from the moment the founder starts to round up support, it is engrained in rituals and symbols, it is put in motion by established work processes and it is at the end a mental model emerging from daily conversations in the (physical or virtual) coffee corner. For ages, this was a slow but steady development process which was rarely affected by, say, the replacement of the CEO or corporate change programs – even if those programs were intended to change the culture. No other quote on the steadiness of corporate culture has been repeated more often than Peter Drucker's culture eats *strategy for breakfast*.

Over the last 20 years however, significant disruptions of the old way of doing things have changed the paradigm that culture doesn't change quickly. Two of those disruptions – digitization and lately, the COVID-19 pandemic – have forced organizations to radically transform and become more responsive to opportunities and threats. We are undergoing the biggest change of global work culture in hundred years, when Alfred P. Sloan invented and implemented the objective organization.

For managers looking for an orientation in the messy situation they find themselves in the age of COVID-19, feeling rather driven by external events than in the driver's seat, this book offers support. And for those asking the question where to start, it gives a clear answer: start anywhere but don't forget to look sideways. *People's* aspirations will not be fulfilled without new *structures*, improved *processes* will not be sustained without adequate *applications*, and new *structures* need new *processes* to support them.

The simplest models are the best. Ute Franzen-Waschke's book helps to get priorities right. That is a good point of departure for the organizational transformations that lie ahead.

Holger Nauheimer

Founder at virtualcollaboration.works

Table of Contents

Preface

The Pre-COVID-19 Era and How Urgency Can Move Paradigms

The COVID-19 Pandemic in 2020 brought a lot of challenges into our lives, and yet it also made space for new paradigms to emerge. One of those paradigm shifts was a changing corporate viewpoint on employees working from home. The battles fought in organizations around the privilege of working from home definitely seemed like a story of the past by mid-2020.

Early in the pandemic, in May 2020, I wrote an article for *Forbes* "On the Precipice of a Culture Shift, Adaptation May Come at Warp Speed" about my observations while working with my clients in multinationals. Over the past decades it had been quite a challenge in some organizations for employees to benefit from the possibility of working from home.

Fear on the corporate side that employees might not be as productive and effective while working from home as well as infrastructure issues, such as insurmountable IT and security concerns, or missing or wrong equipment are just a few of the challenges that kept employers from allowing the average employee to work from home. On the other side there were also concerns among the employees, who wanted to keep their private and working lives strictly separate.

There was also inequality in organizations about who is entitled to the privilege of working from home, if desired. On the one side, there were the organizations that wanted to be trendy and keep or attract talent by offering not just flexible working conditions when it comes to time but also to place. This offered working parents with young children or aging parents the benefit of more flexibility to harmonize their family and working lives. In these organizations, models were offered to some but not to all members of staff. Often it was a matter of position, negotiation skills, or type of work that would open up such possibilities to some.

Studies as far dated back as 2016 demonstrated that working from home definitely had some positive side effects for organizations, with sick leaves and absences from the office going down, and happiness and more positive feelings around work on the staff side going up. Still not everyone was privy to choose freely from where to work.

Then with the urgency of the COVID-19 virus interfering, working from home was all of a sudden seen through a different lens. Economic survival mechanisms helped those with a certain amount of scepticism toward home office work take a different view. Factors such as the strict division between private and working lives as well as the downside of remote work demonstrated in counter studies helped employers swallow the bitter pill and as so often happens, made necessity the mother of invention and creativity.

Without us realizing and taking the time to learn what this "new way of working" actually requires we are finding ourselves head over heels in the midst of it.

To the surprise of many, it has gone much, much better than most would have thought, if asked a few months before the pandemic forced us into this new mode of working. And yet learnings, new experiences, and side effects have also come in fast. But what are organizations doing with these? A common pattern that I have seen in organizations is to continue for as long as possible and for as long as things are running well. The "never change a running system" thinking often gets in the way of reflecting on learning and experiences and prevents true continuous improvement cycles.

Researcher and organizational psychologist David Kolb, who developed the well-

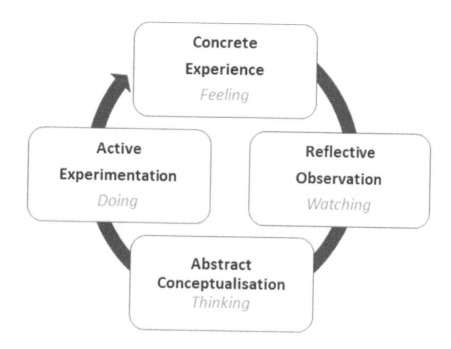

known and respected Kolb Learning Cycle, asserts that knowledge results from the interplay between theory and experience.

Experience alone, according to Kolb, does not necessarily lead to learning and advancement. What is crucial is the critical reflection around the experience. With the **PPAS Maturity Model**®, Kolb's learning cycle comes to life in a participatory and co-creative manner. It focuses on the fact that learning is a cycle and not an achievement, learning goes on and on and on, and with each and every loop there is a chance for improvement and advancement.

The PPAS Maturity Model can be used at various stages of a change process and initiative in corporate settings, but also in the public sector and in education. The particular focus in this book is on working from home during COVID-19 through the corporate lens. The reader will be introduced to the PPAS Maturity Model and its dimensions, will get access to ready-to-use templates to start the conversation with or without a coach at your side, and an overview of how to best navigate through your learnings and experiences in a structured, reflective, and forward-looking manner.

Our avatars Jenn, Laura, and Cynthia will be going through the model with you and will share their personal learnings and reflections along the way. These avatars do not depict any one client in particular that I worked with in 2020 or over the years, but hopefully will help to illustrate and spark thinking around your very personal situations.

My very personal situation also inspired this book and my passion for this topic. Two months before I wrote that aforementioned *Forbes* article, I had relocated with my husband. He had just started an international assignment for his company in the USA only two weeks before COVID-19 forced a lockdown on most countries around the world. Luckily I had been working remotely with coaches and clients from around the globe for many years and so the fact that COVID-19 now required everyone else to work remotely as well didn't distract from my professional/business situation very much.

At the same time, though, as I was convincing my European clients to "travel with me" to the US and to continue to work with me using Zoom instead of meeting them in their offices in Germany, the COVID-19 measures nudged my clients in a catalytic manner to say "yes" to that new way of working, which was great for me, too.

Also at the same time, a colleague of mine, Holger Nauheimer, whom I had known for some years, started an initiative on LinkedIn, which I joined without a second of hesitation. He founded a group called virtualcollaboration.works with experts and change makers from around the globe that also had experience in working in virtual environments. Holger's goal was to help everyone else in these times of change as quickly and as professionally as possible. In less than four weeks Holger and his team set up a virtual conference to do exactly that and it was a huge success.

I had the honor and pleasure to be part of this amazing network of change makers, and helped this conference become a reality both in the back office as well as a face of the conference with workshop offers. One offer was the model that I had already created and used with my clients – at that time it was called the PAS Maturity Model – looking at people, application, and structure. As I was pitching the workshop to Holger and possible participants of the online conference, Holger said that interesting enough he had a similar model, looking at people, tools, and *processes*. After some inspiring conversations and some more hours of personal reflection, the second P for *processes* made it into my model.

The PPAS Maturity Model was presented then again in September during "Changing Conversations for a Changing World," a three-day virtual gathering of the European C-IQ Collective to a small but very enthusiastic audience, who encouraged me to trademark the model (registration is pending) and back it up with research. The research is underway, and when done properly, does take some time and it will continue when this book is already published.

"A journey starts with a first step."

The model, as mentioned before, had already been used and applied with clients before COVID-19 but has become more popular and useful among my corporate clients since then.

Now that my readers know how this model was built and how this book came a reality, we can get ready to take a deeper dive into the dimensions of the model:

People
Processes
Applications
Structure

Who Will Benefit from this Book?

Since I don't know what attracted *you* in particular to this book, what you are hoping to get as insights and inspirations, and what background you are from professionally, I will address some of those professions and likely groups of readers here and will share what my intentions are for you.

Coaches and Consultants

Curiosity and Discovery is my intention for these professions. Going forward after COVID-19, many of your clients will be facing decisions around ways and modes of working, and challenges with co-creating new ways of working. I hope this book and the discovery questions will inspire you to ask more questions for which there are no answers – *yet.*

By raising these questions, you and your clients will be moving closer to these answers – not necessarily immediately due to the complexity and the many voices that you will feel a need to listen to in order to get the full picture. As a coach and consultant, you also come in to help your clients navigate with patience, perseverance, and trust in the process toward success. I wish you every success!

Executives, Leaders, and Employees

Perspectives, openness, and priming for strategic approaches are my intentions for executives, leaders, and employees alike, who are being influenced from the various angles and areas of the organization. Look at working-from-home and working-from-anywhere policies through these different lenses, step into each other's shoes, and see the world through each other's eyes, with the multitude of challenges that are building up within the corporate walls, but also beyond those. Co-creating solutions that support the needs of all parties involved in the best case and in a not-so-perfect world, at least continuously work toward making existing policies better. Continuously apply our experiences and learnings through critical reflections following the Kolb Learning Cycle and use the PPAS Maturity Model as your North Star.

Introduction

How to Read and Use this Book

The four dimensions of the model will be presented in separate chapters. Each chapter will explore in detail what the dimension involves, which discovery questions could be asked, and how these may or may not relate to the three avatars.

After each chapter, you will find templates for you to use and employ when working with the model.

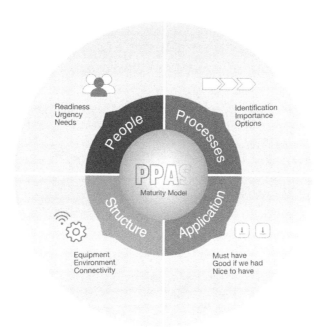

Discover - Analyze - Succeed

Chapter 1

Discovery Questions and the Avatars

What are discovery questions?

Discovery interview questions are questions that allow us to discover and explore a certain topic. Answers to discovery interviews lead to more questions that help to dig deeper and unfold more layers to give more insights around a particular topic. There is no script to a discovery interview other than to co-create it with those people in the room.

In this book, I will share examples for discovery questions that will open a conversation and provide more insights about the needs and gaps around each dimension. These discovery questions will provide answers and insights on the one side and will at the same time also highlight areas that might require deeper and further discovery. The discovery questions I am covering here in this book are mainly focused on remote work and working from home and how to make that migration more sustainable particularly in a post-COVID-19 era.

Meet the Avatars

Senior Management Level

Meet Jenn

Jenn is a senior level executive at an automotive company in Europe and has been with the company for more than ten years. Jenn is a mother of one daughter, Dana, who is in third grade. Jenn's husband works full-time as well in another organization.

Middle Management Level

Meet Laura

Laura is a middle manager. Laura works in customer service at the same automotive company in Europe as Jenn does. Laura is single and looks after her aging parents. Laura has been with the company for twelve years.

Team Member/Working Level

Meet Cynthia

Cynthia works in logistics and has more than fifteen years' experience in the field with the same company. Cynthia's kids are fifteen and eighteen years old. Their names are Jeff and Linda.

Chapter 2

P for People

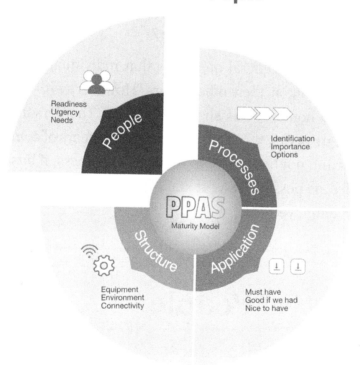

Discover - Analyze - Succeed

Part 1: Meet the dimension

The model starts with the dimension that has the biggest power to either help an initiative to succeed or fail. People are at the center of every change initiative. Their personal **readiness** when it comes to change is a key driver and paired with urgency in the sense of survival.

Questions such as:

- Am I going to keep my job after this change initiative?
- Will I still be capable and able to fulfill what is required and expected of me in the new job, the environment, with the new tasks, new supervisors, colleagues, etc.?
- Will the changes be a benefit for me?
- Will the changes bring any "danger" (job loss, financial drawbacks, etc.) to me or my family?

What is actually in it for me with this change?

The above questions are very general questions that individuals might have when a change initiative is knocking at their office doors. However, with COVID-19 and remote and working from home, it was slightly different. The personal readiness was secondary because the **urgency** was immense. Economic fears of companies that they would lose customers and not being able to remain in business, if businesses couldn't continue as "normally" as possible, was at stake and with that the economic survival of many workers and employees.

People
- Readiness
- Urgency
- Needs

Hence the willingness to be prepared and ready to do something that they might not have done before working from home was something relatively minor in terms of a challenge, compared with the risk to lose work entirely. Only later, when the first COVID-19 wave was over, and some companies were asking their staff to return to their offices, learning, personal preferences, and needs became more relevant and overt than when everyone was in "survival mode" and "coping mode."

COVID-19 has shown both organizations and individuals, who had both been sceptical in the past, that remote work and home office as a concept does work and does not need to be limited to certain privileged groups in the workplace. This realization has allowed space for a more strategic conversation around remote work and working from home policies, which are required at various levels in organisations and in various industries. If companies wanted to really benefit from this excellent learning environment COVID-19 offers them, then following Kolb's research findings would be a good next step.

Now is the time for thorough investigations around what exactly are our learnings on a personal and employee level as well as on a company and organizational level. As Kolb points out, every good reflection, or my preferred phrase in the context of the PPAS Maturity Model – every discovery journey – starts with good questions:

- What did people like when they were working from home?
- Where were they challenged?
- What benefits came from working from home for the organization?
- What challenged the organization?
- What would we as an organization like to keep and offer our staff?
- What would our staff like to keep?
- How can we as an organization co-create with our staff a better work environment that serves multilaterally (company and employee) and not just unilaterally (usually only the company and not the employee)?

Definitely, the answers to these questions will all vary depending on industry, company size, and individual contexts, and might have to be revisited again and again, as things are changing in the respective ecosystem. It's a cycle after all...and learning is not an achievement but something that goes on and on and on...

Let's take a look at some discovery questions for this dimension and then relate them to our avatars and how they experienced them.

People

- How ready is everyone to move from face-to-face to remote?
- What have people enjoyed so far about working remotely?
- What are they going to miss because they enjoy "this" about in-person encounters? How can those misses be compensated or substituted?
- What are people struggling with when working remotely?
- What skills are already there?
- What skills need to be developed?

Part 2: Meet the avatars

Jenn, our senior level executive, was ready right from the start to move from face-to-face to remote. At her level in a large automotive company, she had been used to working from various places around the world. She was used to traveling and working at odd hours due to the international standards of her work. She actually enjoyed it, as it gave her a lot of freedom and flexibility. Jenn has the experience she needs and both access to the technology that is needed to work away from the office desk as well as the skills to master the technology. Jenn had never struggled with any of the requirements that working away from the office had put on her until COVID-19 hit.

During the first lockdown she really learned what it meant to lead a team and a company remotely. When the lockdown began and her organization felt forced to offer working-from-home opportunities to the vast majority of their staff, she had mixed feelings around that initiative, but the leadership team didn't have much choice. It was this or nothing!

The first challenge Jenn personally encountered was that now **remote really meant remote**. There was no possibility at all to meet her peers and her leadership team members, or her direct reports even once in a while. At her level in the organization, however, these inconveniences were handled, she thought, professionally and efficiently.

Another challenge was that all of a sudden Jenn was not working from another location or site of the company, from another office away from her corporate home base, but from her office at home. Luckily, her house was big enough so that she could retract for important calls and work in a focused and concentrated manner. Jenn's husband was suddenly in the same situation and was also working from home. And Jenn's elementary schoolkid, Dana, was now home during the pandemic, and took part in online school sessions and had some school activities to work on without a teacher.

That's when Jenn and her husband needed to come in to support Dana. Jenn and her husband hence had to make arrangements for how to divide up their working day, so that Dana could get the support she needed. This resulted in Jenn and her husband taking turns working late in the evenings or very early in the mornings.

All in all, Jenn still thinks it was a positive experience even though it was exhausting and at times stressful not just professionally but also personally. Going forward as a member of the Senior Leadership team she sees one of her tasks is to come up with a working-from-home strategy in her company.

Some of her Senior Leadership team members see huge savings potential for their organization. The working-from-home strategy worked so well across hierarchies and business units that they could eliminate expensive office space. That would save the company huge amounts of rent every year, and that windfall would come in handy after some challenging years. The automotive sector had been struggling long before the pandemic, with electrification and autonomous driving projects. Now with the pandemic and projects being discontinued or delayed, saving on real estate costs and rent would be a huge relief let alone electricity bills and other utilities, plus coffee, office furniture—and the list is far from being complete.

On the other hand, new working environments had just been created in wonderful office spaces to allow for new methods such as agile work methods. Remote work and working from home are a bit contradictory to hot-desking, daily stand-ups, and short communication ways in open-plan and open space offices.

Laura, our middle manager working in the same company as Jenn, has her own and very personal experience with the People part of the model, and would answer some of the questions differently, others very similarly. For Laura moving from face-to-face to remote work was okay. She had no issues with technology, yet depending on the type of work she did, she missed the proximity to her team leaders and staff.

Customer service work has many interfaces of which some are better handled face-to-face, and so she herself, as well as her team leaders and their staff, were experiencing challenges in the way they were trying to support their clients remotely.

This caused stress and anxieties in the team as well as some disappointments with their customers here and there, as well. Also living alone in her apartment, Laura missed the interaction in the office and felt a bit isolated during the pandemic. Going forward Laura could imagine a healthy mix of working from home as well as from the office. Laura would prefer not having to choose between an either-or system that allowed either work from the office or from home only. A hybrid model would be ideal.

Cynthia is our team member in logistics. Before COVID-19 she had never been allowed to work from home. She didn't even have a laptop. When the pandemic hit and the lockdown started, her employer allowed her to carry her office computer home, something she never thought possible. It was a rough and bumpy start for Cynthia moving her office into her home.

There was the issue of space and the feeling that she was alone with everything. There were no colleagues she could turn to, sitting one or two desks down the hallway, to ask about a tech issue or about a work-related question, nobody to chat with, and no off-the-record information in the coffee kitchen.

Cynthia's husband was home during the lockdown and was on furlough. Cynthia's kids were in a similar situation as Cynthia was: home schooling was an unknown concept to them, and they missed their classmates, as well. Space was a huge issue as three people needed to work from home in a concentrated and focused manner and the internet line simply couldn't cope with the demand, either. It was a stressful time for the entire family when they all started off on this new experience in their home.

Going forward Cynthia could envision working from home for a few days here or there, e.g., when there is bad traffic, heavy snow, or something else going on that would require her presence at home, such as maintenance people coming to service her apartment. In general, however, Cynthia prefers to work from the office.

Template #1: Getting an overview and priming for conversations that matter: Look at each dimension of the model.

Which dimension do **you** think is the most mature in your organization?

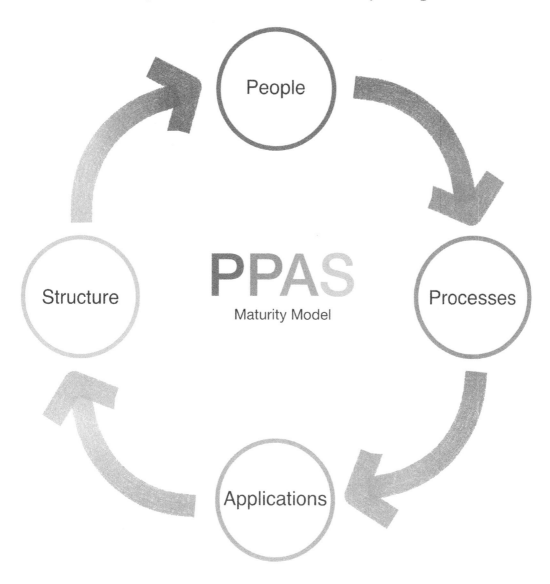

In the left column, check 4 stars for the most mature and 1 star for the least mature.

Next rate the importance for that particular dimension in your organization from 4 stars for very important and 1 star for not important. Do that in the right column.

People

☆ ☆ ☆ ☆

Importance

Processes

☆ ☆ ☆ ☆

Importance

Applications

☆ ☆ ☆ ☆

Importance

Structure

☆ ☆ ☆ ☆

Importance

☆ ☆ ☆ ☆

Template #2: Self-Reflection Employee

For self-reflection to get the thinking process started and for deeper conversations during the workshop if you are preparing for a workshop.

What worked well for you when working from home?

_____
_____
_____
_____
_____
_____
_____
_____
_____
_____
_____
_____
_____
_____
_____

What was challenging?

_____
_____
_____
_____
_____

_____

_____

_____

_____

_____

_____

_____

What are your needs going forward?

_____

_____

_____

_____

_____

_____

_____

_____

_____

_____

_____

_____

How realistic do you think is it that those needs can be covered?
And by whom/and how?

_____

_____

_____

_____

_____

_____

_____

_____

_____

_____

_____

_____

_____

_____

_____

_____

_____

Template #3: Self-Reflection Supervisor

For self-reflection to get the thinking process started and for deeper conversations during the workshop if you are preparing for a workshop.

What worked well for your staff while working from home from your perspective?

_____

_____

_____

_____

_____

_____

_____

_____

_____

_____

_____

_____

_____

_____

What worked well for yourself as a supervisor while working from home?

_____

_____

_____

_____

_____

_____

_____

_____

_____

_____

_____

_____

_____

_____

_____

_____

_____

What was challenging from your perspective for your staff?

_____

_____

_____

_____

_____

_____

_____

_____

_____

_____

_____

_____

_____

_____

_____

_____

_____

What was challenging for you as a supervisor?

_____

_____

_____

_____

_____

_____

_____

_____

_____

_____

_____

_____

What are the needs you identified for your subordinates?

_____

_____

_____

_____

_____

_____

_____

_____
_____
_____
_____
_____

What are the needs you identified for yourself?

_____
_____
_____
_____
_____
_____
_____
_____
_____
_____
_____
_____
_____
_____
_____

What are the needs for the organization?

_____
_____
_____
_____

_____

_____

_____

_____

_____

_____

_____

_____

**How realistic do you think is it that those needs can be covered?
And by whom/and how? What, in your opinion, would be needed?**

_____

_____

_____

_____

_____

_____

_____

_____

_____

_____

_____

_____

_____

Chapter 3

P for Processes

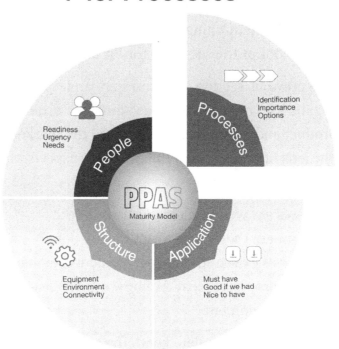

Discover - Analyze - Succeed

Part 1: Meet the dimension

The second *P* for Processes was originally not part of the model. It sneaked in because my colleague Dr. Holger Nauheimer and I had been talking about our models and where they were similar and different, and Holger kept on pointing out the importance of processes in corporate settings. Something I had been well aware of from my work in corporations as well, and yet, for me processes had, until then, come to life with people—the first *P* for People. Processes had, until then, also been covered as an overarching dimension in *S* for Structure and *A* for Applications. I did add the second *P* for Processes as a separate dimension to the Model to acknowledge the importance in organizational settings where, unfortunately, processes often trump people.

In the templates, you will be able to see how these dimensions are correlated and intertwined. People, Applications, Processes, and Structure can never be looked at as stand-alones only. Also, during my talks and presentations of the model in 2020, it indeed turned out that leaders and employees alike thought that the process P bears a lot of food for thought and reflection across organizations and functions, and thus deserved to have its own mentioning. With so much being said about the Process P, let's now take a closer look at the second P for Processes.

As discussed in the previous section, processes are an important part of corporate life – they are road maps for various actions as simple as ordering stationery to how to develop a new product and how to bring it out into the market. When looking at processes through the lens of remote work the following aspects might be a good starting point for the discovery process:

- What processes are we using for our daily work?
- How important are they for us to get the job done?
- What alternatives exist and on which could we fall back, if needed?
- What informal processes exist and how can we be sure not to miss them in a remote work environment?

Once a Process Map has been completed with the respective interfaces, dependencies, and technical requirements mapped out, it is a straightforward yet comprehensive and time-consuming effort to work with the new insights gained and to go through the discovery questions.

One of the challenges will be to work through the interfaces and dependencies to ensure a good transition from "traditional" working models to working-from-home-or-anywhere models.

Processes

- What processes do we need to look at?
- How important are they for us?
- What value do these processes add to what we want and need to accomplish?
- How will these processes be affected by the change from in-person/in-the-room encounters to remonte/virtual work?
- Which processes might have to be reviewed, replaced, or binned?
- What can be simplified and where can we become leaner?

In many organizations certain methodologies, such as agile working methods, e.g. Scrum, with their artifacts, or Design Thinking with its customer or user-centric focus, and any other form of new and inspiring working conditions—all of which shift their focal points to the "people" and their needs when finding solutions to problems in an effective manner—do have considerable impact on the "how" those people can do their jobs. Especially when being forced to work fully remote during the pandemic, employees experienced a major impact on how processes were run and brought to life in different forms and ways than they would have been if their teams could have met, at least for a few days for a face-to-face retreat, in an office or a coworking space.

Tools that would also support these work methods in a virtual environment (which we will look at in more detail in the next dimension, Applications) were priceless for the creativity and were success factors for these new ways of working in a remote environment. However, getting access to what was needed technically from a process point of view was not always that easy. Also providing the training to those who had to work with these new tools and applications to ensure the work processes would continue in an online environment was not always given, and hence lowered productivity and output, taking stress levels and working hours to unhealthy peaks.

Therefore, let's look at the Process P in combination with the previous dimension P for People and also the next dimension, A for Application. But before we move on to Applications, let's turn to our avatars, and read a bit more about how they experienced the P for Processes.

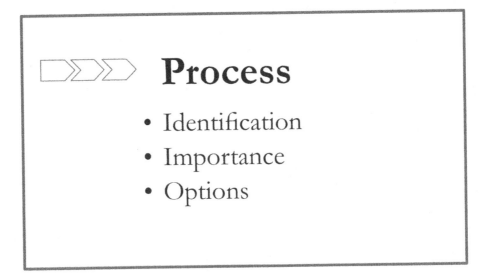

Part 2: What do our avatars think about the P for Processes?

As **Jenn** already reflected in the previous chapter, there seemed to be some challenges in the process landscape of her global automotive employer. Most of the engineering departments completely switched to agile working forms. New workplace designs were invested in, people were trained in agile working methods, and agile transformation projects were either in the midst of implementation or had just been implemented when the pandemic hit.

Now all of these wonderful work areas for stand-up meetings, retrospectives, ad-hoc and impromptu meetings could no longer be used because people were either required to work from home, or because in those open spaces it was much harder to keep up with the hygiene standards necessary to comply with COVID-19 rules and regulations.

Scrum and agile methods can actually work very well in virtual environments, but investments into new tools and applications would be desperately needed so that the same efficient and effective work environments can be replicated in the virtual world. Interactive whiteboards for Post-its and Kanban boards, project management and tracking software that can be moved over to a fully remote team would be needed, as well as the okay from the IT departments, licensing and, even more importantly, the training of staff in the use of these new applications. Very often the latter was neglected.

Learning by doing, experimenter mindsets were taken for granted, but in such a volatile environment, not every employee was an experimenter and had other more burning day-to-day issues to take care of than to work through tutorials to self-learn about new IT applications. In the "good old days" these things had been handled differently and more effectively—that was at least Jenn's honest opinion. Something that definitely needed some more strategic thought and planning was the scanning of the market regarding which tools would work best for their processes. Could those tools be used in their corporate IT environment and from their staff when they were working from home?

Something Jenn needed to bring up at the next Senior Leadership team meeting with CTO, so that a strategy could be worked out and implemented as soon as possible. Even if people would eventually return to their working places for good, it would never be in the same way as before, and remote work would remain a reality to a much larger extent than it used to be before the pandemic.

Laura, our middle manager, was facing some challenges on the operational level with the process landscape now that everyone was all of a sudden working from home. Not every employee who reported to her was used to working remotely. For some team members new processes had just been implemented and, while they had been content and confident executing them while working in the office, now some of her best people were struggling.

Laura would definitely appreciate some guidelines and support on how to train her people in working remotely in an effective and efficient manner, making sure new work processes and workflows were handled with the same confidence and efficiency from those working at home and in collaboration across time zones and geographies. There was definitely a huge improvement potential once everyone would come up for air after the pandemic.

Cynthia, our team member in logistics, was overwhelmed with the new situation of working from home. She hadn't had the chance to reflect at a deeper level on how her processes served or did not serve the new working environment. From the outside it seemed to be working. But the extra time, effort, and stress this all had taken was beyond the limits of acceptance.

Getting through hurdles and to secure the authorizations she needed from a process delegate point of view for the three new projects she was now working on may sound like a simple step in a process, but was anything like that in reality. She was hugely grateful for the support and understanding she got from the IT people on the hotline, as well as her manager. Now that everything seems to be working, at least from what Cynthia could see, she still had doubts deep inside. Who knows, she often was saying to herself. It works smoothly now, but one does not know what one doesn't know. Maybe this is just an illusion and the big bang is yet to come.

With the big bang, Cynthia meant anything the systems were or were not doing and which would show up in another part or segment of the process chain and would then become a problem for all, but at a stage when it might already be too late to fix. Nevertheless, Cynthia continued with her work rhythm in the same way, following the flowcharts and work instructions. When encountering an issue, she turned to her supervisor, who at times was challenged by her questions, too, but stayed calm for most of the time.

Things were moving a tiny bit slower but at least they were moving, and she could make sure that both internal and external customers continued to be happy with the delivery performance of the logistics department of which she is a member.

Other aspects when looking at processes in a remote work context were to revisit meeting schedules, meeting protocols, feedback loops, and communication channels. Topics, which had always been on the agenda of a project kickoff when working from the office, even then, didn't get the attention that they should have.

Now Cynthia had the feeling that these omissions were coming back on everyone even harder. Remote workplaces do need their own special rules of engagement, ways of working – and since nobody really had fallen in love with those in the real world, it was even harder to convince supervisors that they were desperately needed now more than ever in the virtual world.

Especially the informal pat on the shoulder, the words of appreciation and recognition received in the coffee corner or in an informal conversation in the office; the kind of feedback that keeps the engagement and motivation engine of every employee going, seemed to be dying out or at least needed a reviving impulse in the virtual workplace.

The idea of having a performance review conversation or maybe a difficult conflict-loaded conversation with a supervisor, project leader or HR person in a remote environment rather than in an office was a thought that made Cynthia frown. Her impression was that these types of conversations had already been challenging when they took place face-to-face and were at times avoided for the exact same reason. What would that mean in the long run for these types of essential conversations if they were to take place in the virtual environment?

How much more often would they then be avoided or skipped under the veil of busyness?

Processes

Template #4: Process Audit

For ratings we use the star model

4 stars – max. rating, 1 star – min. rating

Name of the Process	Brief Description	Importance	My maturity mastering the process	Maturity of the process	Suitability for remote work

☆ ☆ ☆ ☆

Template #5: Meeting Audit

For ratings we use the star model

4 stars – max. rating; 1 star – min. rating

Template #6: Communication Channel(s)

For ratings we use the star model

4 stars – max. rating; 1 star – min. rating

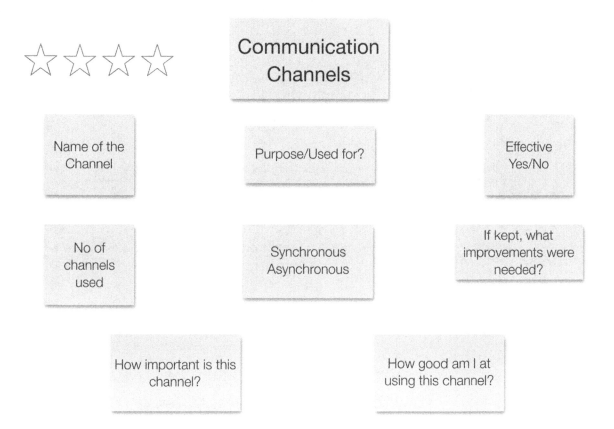

A first example for how to link Processes with Structures and to find dependencies/ interfaces between **Processes** and Structures. This example and more of that kind can be revisited at the end of Chapter 5 - S for Structure.

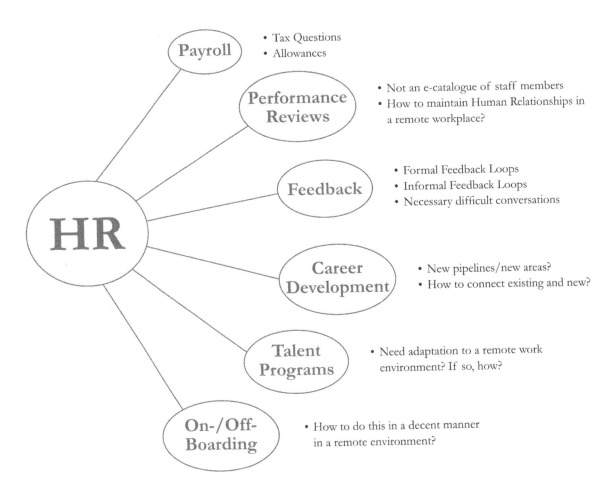

You can add more satellite bubbles, rename them, and remove them as needed...it's only a beginning...these are your ideas and your structures and processes!

Chapter 4

A for Applications

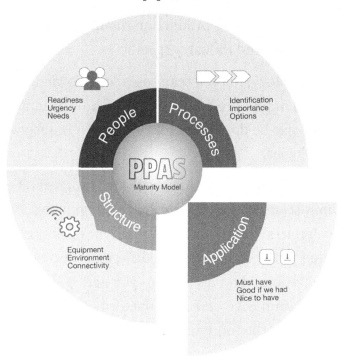

Discover - Analyze - Succeed

Part 1: Meet the dimension

Applications are the tools we use on our desktop computers, laptops, and mobile devices to help us do our jobs more efficiently on the one side, and on the other side are important windows and gateways to connect with team members and colleagues, especially when working from anywhere or remotely from home. In this dimension when we are talking about applications, we go beyond the apps described above and also include any software tools that help those at work to do their jobs. One huge application that is included in this is SAP. As without SAP many work processes would not be possible. Included in that is also the MS Office Suite 365, Atlassian tools, and any other digital helpers that make lives at work easier, more efficient, and effective.

The tools and applications that are used at work every day are often connected with the *P* for processes. As processes are often supported by highly customized computer tools and applications that help employees with the administrative side of their job, as well as in the production and manufacturing field to help navigate and steer supply mechanisms, monitor quality, and production quantities, the dimension of Applications is often very company and industry specific.

Thanks to modern technology, not only can so-called knowledge workers or office staff work from home, but maintenance of machines and adjustments in programs for production machines can also be done remotely, thanks to Industry 4.0 or SmartFactory principles and technologies.

Applications such as Outlook, Word, and Excel are standard office applications without which the administrative work would be unimaginable. On the manufacturing side, however, a wider array of highly customized applications has been streamlined for a successful segue to the aforementioned Industry 4.0/SmartFactory principles. Microsoft and SAP have joined forces and are partnering more and more on integrating Microsoft products into SAP and manufacturing applications with the focus on making collaboration smoother and more seamless.

Whereas Slack, Trello, Mural, Miro, ideaclouds, and project management or tracking applications such as Monday.com and Asana are only slowly moving into the official office world, at least with the big multinationals whose IT departments are powerful and have the difficult task to keep their intranets safe, as well as all transactions within their sphere of responsibility.

Zoom, Wonder and Co with their amazing Breakout Room and networking features, in which real open space working environments can be transferred into the virtual world in an easy and efficient manner, have an even harder time making it into the corporate world. At the top of my list of favorite virtual collaboration platforms is and remains Howspace.

Some IT departments say these fantastic tools cannot be used because of security issues, others are more honest and admit that there are cost and licensing reasons as well behind their resistance. My experience was that the latter, namely cost and licensing fees, are the more realistic and honest reasons, but hardly ever spoken out loud. The cost discussion is indeed understandable, because it does add up when a company needs to buy licenses for all their staff, for example, so they are able to arrange meetings in Zoom, to create a Whiteboard/Interactive Board in Miro, Mural, or with IdeaClouds, that can be accessed by all team members.

The MS Office Suite, which offers most of the above in just one package – yes, with certain limitations when it comes to user-friendliness and feature effectiveness – but scoring for companies when it comes to economic reasons because of their all-inclusive approach, and their omnipresence in companies and corporations around the globe. Also, the free-of-charge applications of the Google Suite are very easy to use and freely accessible, but are often banned from corporate IT environments for data security reasons.

However, why these very useful and highly effective applications such as Zoom or Wonder cannot be used when offered by externals at no costs or at a nominal tech fee, is something that was hard to understand in the beginning. And the security issues that were often brought forward, at least in the beginning for – from the outside perspective – no real reason, put a bad light on the respective applications and hindered to a certain extent effective and efficient collaboration while working from home.

Thankfully, at the beginning of 2021, restrictions have been loosened even in the most conservative and security-conscious companies, which does lead to a confirmation of the assumption that security cannot have been their major concern from the start. Zoom has also worked relentlessly in 2020 to prove how safe and secure their tool is.

The conversation around which tools we have that allow remote work at an effective and efficient level gains traction and is growing in importance. Also, how adept is the workforce in organizations in using the tools they have at their disposal? What training needs are there to be fulfilled, and how do organizations best cover these to maximize output with the tools already in place?

Which tools do organizations need to open up when going forward with remote work in a serious manner? What gap would they close and how important is it to close that gap?

Which tools can we allow our staff to benefit from when an external consultant offers them for a workshop or a project?

Which tools do really have security issues and must therefore be avoided and forbidden?

Serious conversations...let's not procrastinate having them because they mean an increase in productivity and effectiveness on the corporate side, and workplace satisfaction on the human and workforce side. So, a win-win at both ends.

⬇ ⬇ Applications

- Which tools do we need for our new virtual work environment? Are they available in the company? If not, could we get access to them?
- What tools are already in use and how useful are they really? (Keep it, Change it, Bin it?)
- If there were no internal restrictions from IT side - company wise - which tools would you add, what benefits would they bring, and what are the costs involved as well as the training needs on the user/employee side?

Check out the templates at the end of this chapter, so you can start with an Application audit and gain clarity, looking at immediate, midterm, and longer-term solutions.

Those templates provide a useful discussion basis for this highly relevant topic and are fully customizable.

Applications

- Must have
- Good if we had
- Nice to have

Part 2: What do our avatars think about the A for Applications?

Jenn sees the entire situation around the pandemic as a great opportunity to liberate the use of applications in the entire company. In her role and in her business area she would have loved to introduce some digital whiteboards, virtual collaboration platforms, and Scrum/agile tools that would not just support remote work in a more productive way but also would be *fun* to use while working from the office. After all, her engineering managers are mostly dispersed across the globe, and most standups do take place across geographic borders and time zones.

How handy would a virtual whiteboard be to capture not just the thoughts of those who participated in the stand-ups in the morning, but when it's online, the next team could see right away and take those contributions and continue to expand on them. Work-arounds with photos, Excel sheets, and other "substitute applications" have done the trick, but there are so many more cool tools and applications out there, that had been off-limits before COVID-19, and still are not within the comfort zone of the CTO and the IT department.

But at least they seem to be opening up to those a little bit, due to the pressure and the need of internal and external facilitators who are hired to plan and design workshops that now go over more than three or four hours – sometimes even a day – and can now only be done in virtual environments. With that prerequisite comes the need to allow tools that also encourage participation and involvement by each and every workshop participant in such a remote world.

Thank goodness her company has some excellent external service providers on their supplier list, who not only have licensed the use of these tools, but also know how to use them effectively. Jenn has encouraged her direct reports to use these external service providers wherever necessary to make sure staff and customers can achieve what it takes to get the product on the market.

That means money for her company – and the job done in the best possible manner, and hopefully future new business with that customer, even under these challenging economic circumstances – especially with the added levels of difficulty that a remote work environment puts on those expectations.

Jenn hopes that dipping the company's toes into those waters with these fun and highly efficient and effective tools will set the stage for necessary changes for a time after COVID-19, or at least opens up a conversation around those applications that would be really nice to have going forward.

Laura would see some need for an application audit and for strategic decisions on topics such as: use of tools, training of staff, and what the long-term goal of the company will be when it comes to remote work. Some of Laura's direct reports have continuously received questions from their staff about a work-from-home policy, with guidelines when it comes to use of tools, especially the use of video, attendance, core work time with kids being homeschooled, weekend work, and work ethics in general.

It seems as though the use of video has risen in comparison to when people were working from the office. Despite this trend, some employees are struggling because they see the use of video as an intrusion into their private sphere on the one side, and on the other side, they see the benefit of seeing each other when working together during the pandemic. Building relationships when the camera is on does help a lot, while difficult conversations can also be done in a less intimidating and more connecting way when the video is on.

Yet, there are also country-specific rules and limitations to that, which need to be considered and accepted – at least for now. If, however, working from home would one day become the "new normal" Laura feels that company rules and guidelines should trump those local regulations because of some of the proven benefits of seeing each other and working together with the camera switched on.

In a global workforce no member of the team should be disadvantaged or should fear any legal trouble because of the agreed ways of working—another reason to advocate the use of a separate room to which the door can be closed when working from home or anywhere. Engagement levels will go up, too, with the camera switched on. Of that Laura is convinced, as well.

Her direct reports have demanded more transparency and clarity about which tools are okay for them to use and which aren't. There seems to be some confusion and definitely different voices in the company. IT after all has stricter points of view than some managers, who clearly see the benefit of certain tools and feel inclined to allow them, so that productivity and efficiency can be kept up with the demands that working from home put on their staff. They are, in some cases, moving in a gray area and risk being reprimanded and that does not feel like a good place to be operating from.

Laura feels that decisions in lower hierarchal levels are taken on the basis of gut feeling, but not in a strategic manner. Senior management is avoiding certain important decisions – at least that's what it feels like for her. From her point of view, an application audit, which would be a guided and structured conversation around the use of tools and applications, would be highly beneficial.

Cynthia really had a hard time getting used to working 100 percent remotely. In the past she did connect with her colleagues worldwide on a regular basis but still had her colleagues on-site and in her open plan office that she could refer to, as well. Also the technical hotline was constantly busy during the pandemic—no surprise—because *everyone* was nowadays calling them and needing their support.

Cynthia was empathetic with the hotline staff and yet got frustrated from time to time when her work was delayed because of missing tech support. Sometimes she did call a colleague, as she would have done in the office, but they were busy getting their work done, too. Some processes simply took longer, now that everyone was finding their way in being fully remote.

Cynthia's team leader was a huge support. He was very understanding for the challenges the entire team was facing and was grateful for all the extra effort everyone was putting in to meet the deadlines and to keep customers as happy as one could under these challenging circumstances.

Cynthia's group leader also had a great idea and created a virtual coffee corner where team members could just pop in when they felt they needed company or a break from the treadmill, which wasn't spent alone in the kitchen at home or in the living room or on the balcony. The tool the team members used was not an official company tool. Therefore, one could only meet in that coffee corner from a private device using a link that her team leader had created on a private device with a private account.

The coffee corner was a place that saved some souls and kept the spirits high when stress levels were high, too, and social contacts due to lockdown were low. Usually after work, the coffee corner was a good place to unwind...similar to walking to the parking lot together with a colleague in the good old days when everyone was working from the office. What a great initiative of Paul's, Cynthia's team leader, and what a pity that only her team benefitted from this awesome idea – at least from what Cynthia knew. This would be a cool tool, and Cynthia would definitely recommend it as a nice-to-have tool going forward, if indeed the company decided to continue working from home for a longer time or even forever.

Something Cynthia would also definitely highlight in an applications/tools audit was the need for proper training when it comes to the use of new tools. Absolutely essential if a company goes 100 percent remote. However, from the bottom of her heart, Cynthia hoped that her team and her employer would be open for an on-demand remote work policy once life would be back to normal again. On the other side, Cynthia continued to think how, when life would be "normal" again, she could also meet with her colleagues outside of work, as they did in the virtual coffee corner.

But then again, she had her doubts if everyone would be as committed to spending their private time together in normal times as they were now in these special times in order to compensate for the lack of workplace socializing. In other countries, such as the UK for example and Australia, she had heard from colleagues that they would go out for a drink after work on a regular basis before COVID-19 or they would play soccer together in a park during an extended lunch break a few times a week. That sounded like a normal part of their working life traditions and rituals, but not as much in Germany, where there was a stricter distinction between working time and private time. After all, one would possibly prefer meeting friends again and relatives in their private time once COVID-19 was more under control.

Still, it would remain important as well for a work team to spend time together not just on work topics and tasks, but Cynthia was not going to spend too much thought on that right now, as this all seemed really too far off a look into the future.

Applications Audit/Tool Audit

For ratings we use the star model

4 stars – max. rating; 1 star – min. rating

Template #7: Tools available in-house (Must have)

Tools made available by external coaches, facilitators, contractors, etc…

For ratings we use the star model

4 stars – max. rating; 1 star – min. rating

Template #8: Tools available in-house (Good to have)

Good if we had

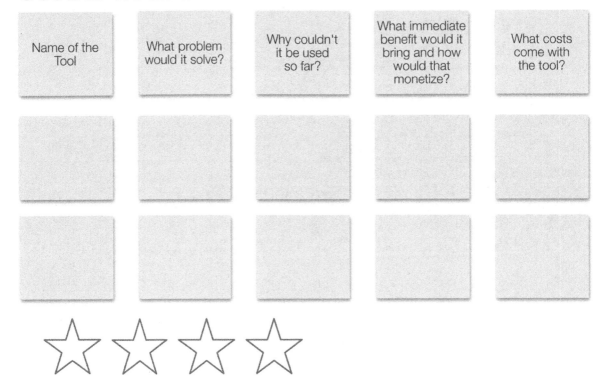

Tools that are off-limits for in-house use but would be nice to have in-house

For ratings we use the star model

4 stars – max. rating; 1 star – min. rating

Template #9: Tools available in-house (Nice to have)

Nice to have

Name of the Tool	What problem would it solve?	Why couldn't it be used so far?	What immediate benefit would it bring and how would that monetize?	What costs come with the tool?

☆ ☆ ☆ ☆

Chapter 5

S for Structure

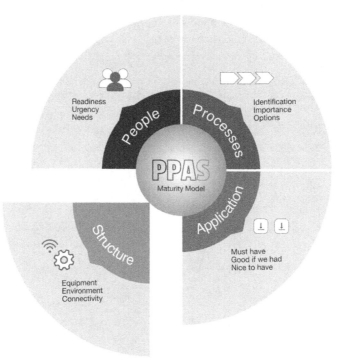

Discover - Analyze - Succeed

Part 1: Meet the dimension

Structure/Infrastructure is another dimension – apart from the first one, People – that is very important in this conversation and often leaves the biggest room for discovery. In those conversations that I had both with staff and management in 2020 during the time of the pandemic, this dimension was rated as the one with the lowest levels of maturity. The dimension of Structure/Infrastructure is also one where companies have only a limited sphere of influence, at least the way things were set up in 2020 during the emergency mode from which many organizations were operating.

Structure on the one side, is the internal organizational structure, and Infrastructure on the other side, depends as well on where people live, how people live, and what family situation they are in. If the impact 'structure' (more precisely here infrastructure) makes on the overall success of corporate remote work can be changed to a more positive one going forward depends to a large extent on whether or not cities and providers can ramp up their endeavours to provide better infrastructure from a technical point of view, and whether or not governments will be there to support the necessary developments in communities, schools, and urban development. This is a crucial dimension when it comes to success or failure when working from home, not just for employees but also for communities and municipalities to consider when attracting citizens to live there.

During the pandemic there were mixed messages around moving from cities to the countryside. It seemed safer in the countryside, since more distance could be kept there than in the cities, but the downside was that often the broadband internet which is so badly needed to work from anywhere wasn't always available at the desired rate.

Another aspect of this dimension is the way people live. Are they a single household and do they have the liberty in using their private space as they please and need it? Or is it a family household in which different needs need to be catered to? How spacious are the living quarters to allow for each and every family member to work in a quiet place in a focused manner?

At the workplace one could look at this dimension also through the lens of "how are we structured?" Where do we have structures, such as meeting structures, general assemblies for the workforce, election processes for participatory organs such as trade unions, work councils etc., and how are these influenced by a remote workforce?

When looking at the work environment of the employee who is working from home a checklist could look like this:

- Does the employee have a separate room that could be used as an office? Where is the desk located? In a separate room, where a door can be closed?
- How is the internet connection in that region/area?
- How many in the household are sharing and using this internet connection at the same time?
- Does the employee have all the necessary hardware to work from home – laptop or desktop computer, printer, scanner, etc.?
- Does the employee have access from home to all the tools or applications they need in order to work efficiently and effectively?

Another important item to reflect on in this dimension is how experienced the employee is in working from home? Do they have the ability to structure their day with the distractions that may occur when working from home – family members, ringing private landlines, doorbells etc. – as well as to keep up a professional attire when attending internal meetings and even more important when attending meetings with customers and clients?

 Infrastructure

- When people should work from home do they have enough bandwidth where they live?
- Is there a quiet room at home to work from?
- Does everyone have the hardware necessary for that? If not, is there any corporate budget to sponsor equipment for the home office work place?
- What is 'necessary' (as hardware) to work effectively from home?
- Does everyone have access to everything (files, sites, machines, equipment) they need for their job also while working from home?
- What extra requirement does that put on IT security aspects?
  Is IT prepared for that? What does the client/quality department say about that job/position moving to a home office place?
- What do trade unions/works councils and the labour law say about home office work places?

Has the employee the ability and support from their supervisors to reinforce a workday structure to ensure when and how to start or end the actual working day and to stay away from the computer? It can be very tempting to work at odd hours, especially when there is time pressure in projects and jobs need to get done with a pressing deadline pushing.

What mechanisms are in place to prevent tensions between bosses working in different time zones and setting up meetings at normal times of their working day but at odd times of the day for those working in different time zones? This is not an entirely new challenge for globally dispersed teams, however, during the COVID-19 lockdown in 2020 it was observed that meetings were called at more odd times of the day because "people were at home anyway." The boundaries were harder to keep by the employees and easier to overcome by supervisors.

How much understanding is there on both sides for saying no or not attending a meeting even if the computer is just next door? What are the expectations with these new possibilities on both sides of the table? What is expected from the employee and what will management allow or limit, also keeping their social corporate responsibility in mind?

What do we need to consider with regard to:

- connectivity and broadband capacity at home
- hardware employee has access to
- availability of the employee when working from home?

How can we negotiate and co-create rules of engagement when working from home between employees, supervisors, customers, clients, and management?

Co-creating rules of engagement among team members and in alignment with management of how and when to work in this new time and setup bear huge opportunities, such as high levels of flexibility to work and align on the employee side. For example, to maybe support and help kids that attend school from home, or taking turns with spouses, who also work from home, as well as on the employer side when it comes to working at times that suit co-workers in other time zones better and weren't so easy to accommodate when work took place in the traditional setting from the office during local office hours.

However, these flexible models during COVID-19 times were also prone to a huge potential for loss of trust again between employee and supervisor, or even up to management level – namely, when people do not seem "available" during the traditional "core office hours" as they were defined during working-from-the-office times, or when work packages were delayed or not delivered. Certainly, the latter could have happened as well during traditional working-from-office times, but there, "commitment" was taken more for granted than "when the staff is working from home" and "out of sight." Easily old patterns keep on creeping in again—justified or not.

However, when a co-created agreement on a working day structure has been negotiated and is communicated in a transparent manner to all parties involved, falling back to these old thinking patterns about working-from-home loss of productivity myths will be kept at bay to a certain extent, and will put the minds of all involved into a more settled and safe space.

Rules can also be easier reinforced on both sides, employee and employer, when they are in place and known across the workforce, helping black sheep from spoiling the whole experience for those who are playing by the rules, not just in working-from-home times but in general.

It would also put HR minds more at ease by respecting labor law and trade union agreements and still allowing an employee to participate in a meeting that takes place in the evening because of time differences with co-workers. They can do so because they took a longer lunch break to support the kids or ran errands or took care of chores around the house. Logging in at odd times of the day wouldn't result in bad conscience anymore and for anyone, neither employees nor supervisors.

As with everything, there are always two sides to the coin. The downsides of these structural flexibilities could lie in the different living situations of each employee:

- When the employee does not have a separate room and needs to work from the kitchen or dining room table, then there is the risk again of inequality. The employee who has a separate room could offer this flexibility to his supervisor and the company might see it as a benefit and value the employee more than the employee who doesn't have a separate room and can't offer that flexibility.

- What if an employee experiences higher levels of stress because of the working-from-home situation and the expectations to be managed around this often unresolved and defined new workplace situation?
- How and where can an employee get support with any of the challenges that they cannot address with their immediate supervisor or where there is a lack of understanding on the side of the supervisor?
- How can tensions be addressed and expectations be managed in a healthy way when we are not working in the same workplace physically?

The dimension of Structure/Infrastructure therefore also connects with internal company structures, which again often correlate to the Process P, when looking, for example, at meeting structures and communication processes.

From a strategic point of view and assuming a corporate intention to pursue a working-from-home or working-from-anywhere strategy that goes beyond and is carried over successfully beyond the time of the pandemic, the dimension of Structure/Infrastructure needs to be explored with both dimensions People and Processes in mind and in view.

The correlation and interconnectedness of these are too significant to look at each in isolation only. One can for sure start by looking at each of them, but then needs to join the dots on a larger scale to ensure that both organizations and employees thrive, even if they do in different parts of their lives and at different levels. One influences the other.

Organizations are looking to thrive economically. Employees are looking to thrive not just economically, i.e. by making the money they need to make a living and to survive, but also how much they like to do their work (job satisfaction), how good they feel about the work they do (sensemaking and purposeful), the difference they make (fulfilment), and the team members they collaborate and co-create with (social contacts and bonds).

These very personal needs and individual circumstances help organizations and staff to see clearer for whom working from home or from anywhere could actually work in the long run—and how to make it a win-win for both employee and employer. And, of course, for the customers as well, whom we should not forget in this relationship, as they are the economic justification of the company's existence.

So-called "hybrid" solutions, solutions in which a company offers both models, working from home or anywhere and coming to the office, seem intriguing and might look like a covering-all-bases model, but could bring an added level of difficulty. Again, questions would arise such as: why can some work from home or anywhere and why others can't? Who decides? Is there a must work from office or work from home policy for some but not for others?

Relationship building and maintaining would also be more challenging if some staff work in the office and another part of the workforce works from home or anywhere.

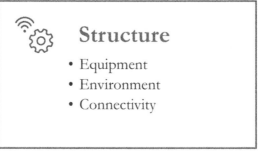

Structure

- Equipment
- Environment
- Connectivity

What about promotions and career planning?

A hybrid model would definitely require more careful considerations of its many facets. The either remote or office model would bear advantages and disadvantages for both workforce and organizations. Another indicator that more conversations need to take place between the stakeholders to craft the model that works best for everyone, taking their particular circumstances and the structural prerequisites and conditions into consideration, with the opportunities and limitations that are in place.

During the conversations I had in 2020 across hierarchies, so many different aspects played a role in job satisfaction, productivity, and happiness both professionally and personally that any other dimension can be worked out somehow, but People and Structure need to be looked at with particular attention.

Organizations and governments around the world are also invited to talk about how their legal constructs either support or hinder these flexible working concepts. One topic, for example, that kept on coming up in my conversations with employees in particular in 2020 was the fact that companies could see huge saving potentials when it comes to office space and rent, electricity, and other overhead costs. Whereas electricity bills for private individuals were rising because of working-from-home situations during the pandemic. The same happened for those employees who upgraded their Wi-Fi plans with their internet providers in order to allow for more stable internet connections during video calls and multiple users taking bandwidth from the connection during the day in the same household.

Lucky were those whose provider could offer them more bandwidth. Frustrated and stressed were those who lived in areas where that was not an option. Frustrated and stressed as well were those who didn't have the financial means to buy that extra connectivity power. Nothing that might have affected those in our view now, but certainly those who lost their jobs, working short time or on furlough with kids being homeschooled and still having higher demands on internet broadband structures with their kids.

In Germany, there also used to be a lot of discussions around inequality for tax write-offs among certain professions. Before the pandemic, only certain professions were eligible to deduct costs for a room used as an office in their private homes and households. There are, of course, certain requirements connected with such a room to make it tax deductible, e.g., it has got to be a separate room, and can't be a desk in a dining room or kitchen.

If these eligible professions had a separate room, then the square meters of that room had a certain percentage tax deductible in terms of rent, electricity, telephone and internet bill, etc. However, ordinary employees, who cannot deduct anything as their workplaces, whose locations that were defined in their employment contracts, were until last year, not eligible for tax benefits or deductions.

Following these discussions, the German government decided to offer employees in 2020 a so-called "Home Office Allowance" of five euros extra per day per employee working from home, with a maximum allowance of 600 euros in total. If that amount will indeed cover the extra effort employees had in 2020, I don't know. Especially, since not just employees but also their kids, who were being schooled from home, contributed to higher expenses in that budget item and are not compensated for in any way through the tax reports.

This "quick tax fix" will at least help to decrease inequality in some areas, but definitely does not go far enough. Again, thinking long-term, governments and organizations are invited to collaborate on a more solid and thought-through strategy that especially ensures that employees of one company, no matter where around the world they work, are treated in an equal opportunity way.

Ideas to layer salaries of those working from home or anywhere based on the location and the connected costs of living does not sound like an employer-friendly solution to me.

Taxation could also, long-term, be an issue. Let's just imagine the following scenario: a knowledge worker has a working-from-anywhere contract with a German multinational and decides to work from another European country, such as Spain during the winter and Austria in the summer—no big deal from work permit point of view and taxation point of view. However, what if the employee decides to work from Australia, the USA, the Caribbean, or Mexico instead? Would that be possible from a working time/availability during office hours point of view looking through the corporate lens, and what would that mean for work permits, payroll, and taxation from an employee's point of view?

The dimension of Structure/Infrastructure is a very complex one and does not end at the door of the organization, but continues on to the homes of the employees, the cities, and countries the companies are based in and the employees live in.

Part 2: What do our avatars think about the S for Structure?

Jenn and her husband had worked out a detailed plan on how to juggle their work commitments and the responsibilities they felt toward a third grader who was being homeschooled for most of the year in 2020. The few weeks that Dana had gone to school in 2020 opened up a window for Jenn and her husband to aspire what working from home or working from anywhere could look like, if only employees would be working from home but not *everyone*. Once kids would go back to kindergartens and schools that would release some of the tensions and stress in some households.

And since it wasn't easy for Dana not to have contact with any of her friends at school, and since even the majority of the teachers were struggling with their new teaching environment, it was clear to Jenn and her husband that they wanted to support Dana as well as they could by organizing their schedules in such a way that it would benefit the entire family. They were both aware and grateful that they had the luxury and privilege of doing so, which came with their positions in the companies they were working for.

Both Jenn and her husband were in positions that were demanding on their working hours, but also allowed a certain level of autonomy and flexibility. Nobody would give them a strange look if they worked at odd hours of the day, e.g. late in the evenings or early in the mornings in order to make up for time they wanted to spend or had spent with Dana during the day. As long as they were present in their mandatory work meetings, available spontaneously when their peers or subordinates needed a quick piece of information or an approval click, and delivered on what they had promised to deliver. This definitely was different in less senior positions in the company, and also in other companies in general.

Another advantage Jenn and her family had was the spacious house they lived in. Plenty of rooms to find a quiet and peaceful place to work in a focused and concentrated manner for every family member. A garden to relax and catch some fresh air in between online meetings and conferences. Both in her husband's as well as in her organization, she had heard of much more challenging family situations. At school as well, during the past virtual parental meeting, the challenges society was facing had become obvious to Jenn and her husband, and so she was even more grateful that this was something her family didn't have to worry about and struggle with.

The position Jenn had in the company allowed her to start a conversation around how to best support efforts that would help ease these struggles for employees in her organization – something HR should be looking into going forward.

Laura could see the structural challenges that Jenn had only heard of among her direct reports and their team members. Many of them were facing difficulty in restructuring their days in the many different constellations that were out there. The family fight around bandwidth, computer time if not everyone in the family had a computer, and a quiet place to work or do homework from.

These were constant topics in their team check-ins. Some of her direct reports were exhausted themselves and others felt helpless toward their team members whose struggles they could see but didn't know how to support them. Especially with the many deadlines they were facing themselves and with everyone working from home, some things did indeed take longer. They got done on time, but getting there was sometimes more time-consuming.

The whole situation around working from home took a toll on some families more than others, that was for sure. How to compensate and cater for that as a supervisor was something she would love to get more support and guidance with from both her direct supervisor and from HR, the works council, and whoever else could ease some of the challenges and signs of exhaustion.

Leading in a virtual environment definitely needed different skill sets and there was an undeniable training need for that. Moreover, guidelines around the reliefs she was allowed to offer to those that she felt were struggling the most were lacking. Nothing could be worse in the current situation than if the company lost experienced staff and talents in those difficult times because of burnout and exhaustion, or maybe because other companies were faster adapting and catering for their employees' new needs.

For Laura herself, structural issues were actually no issues. As a single she had her apartment to herself and also didn't have to share her internet line with a teenager or a partner. She also enjoyed the freedom to visit her aging parents more often during the pandemic than she would have if she had been working from the office.

Cynthia felt some of the infrastructural challenges in her family. Thank goodness her company had given her a computer right at the start of the working-from-home movement. The family computer she shared with her husband wouldn't have done the trick. Both kids had laptops, not the latest models but still they each had one, and their smartphones. They were quite adept at using technology, something Cynthia felt entirely grateful for.

Her eighteen-year-old graduated in the summer of the pandemic and, oh man, that was a hard time. Cynthia and her husband offered a lot of mental support for her eighteen-year-old. The fifteen-year-old needed motivation to stay on top of things and needed help to structure his day at home managing schoolwork. How good it was that her husband had some extra time to keep an eye on them, as Cynthia was busy getting herself and her job organized from her new home office.

The internet connection was a constant cause for worry. The teens sometimes used their smartphones as hot spots but that simply ate up their data volume, which they needed to stay in touch with their friends during the lockdown and which they didn't want to sacrifice for school. Quite understandable at that age.

What a relief it was for Cynthia when her boss offered a Vodafone GigaCube to help with the internet struggles she was experiencing in her household. The cube was a hot spot hardware device that would give Cynthia a personal Wi-Fi line that she could use for work purposes only.

The extra money she would have to invest in a better line for her private household would take time, as the providers in her area didn't have much to offer at this point and would also be hard on the family financially with her husband, the main bread-winner of the family, being on furlough.

This example was already shown after Chapter 3 in - P for Processes, and more examples were promised after Chapter 5 - S for Structure. Here they are:

For ratings we use the star model

4 stars – max. rating; 1 star – min. rating

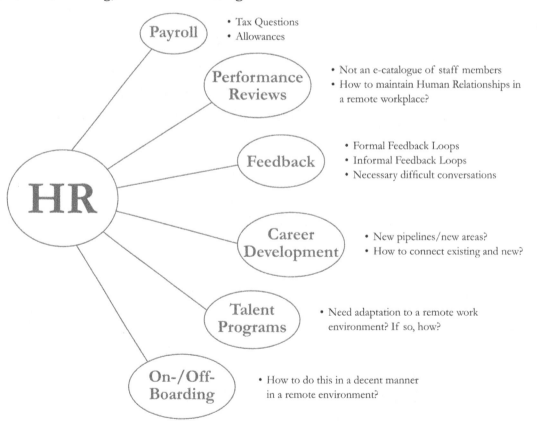

You can add more satellite bubbles, rename them and remove them as needed...it's only a beginning...these are your ideas and your structures and processes!

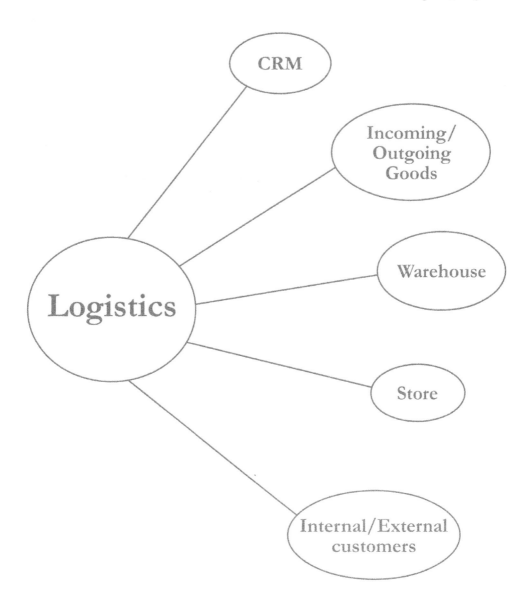

You can add more satellite bubbles, rename them and remove them as needed…it's only a beginning…these are your ideas and your structures and processes!

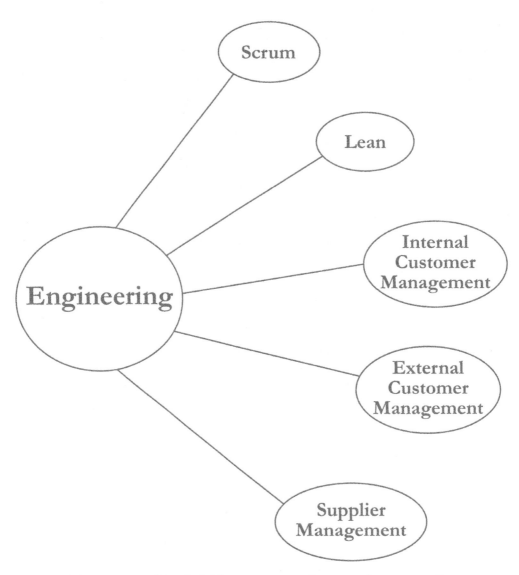

You can add more satellite bubbles, rename them and remove them as needed...it's only a beginning...these are your ideas and your structures and processes!

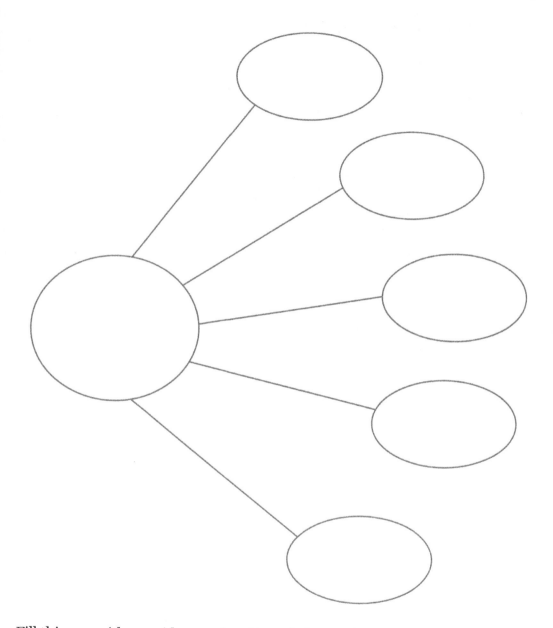

Fill this one with your ideas and replicate it for as often as needed...

Template #10: Structure/Infrastructure

Infra-Structure

Questions for the organization

Does the effort (of moving this place to a home office place) match the benefit? Whose benefit?

Are customer/clients okay with this role moving to a home office work place?

Who else needs to be involved in this conversation that hasn't been involved yet?

What roles/positions/jobs can work from home/anywhere?

Work contracts - What needs to be amended/added/removed?

Distinction between working from home and working from anywhere?

Can staff access everything they need also from home/anywhere?

What special equipment does staff need to work from home/anywhere?

Can staff use their private internet line?

What equipment is necessary to work from home/anywhere?

Chapter 6

Before You Leave...

...let me say thank you for showing an interest in the PPAS Maturity Model and for being curious to learn more about yet another, different approach to change processes and change initiatives. There are already many out there, so I truly and honestly appreciate your perseverance in trying to find the Holy Grail. Not that the PPAS Maturity Model is trying to be that.

Maybe you were looking for orientation and guidance in the jungle of remote work and hopefully you have found a little bit of that.

Maybe you have read this in preparation for a workshop or a series of workshops we are embarking on together as part of an engagement with your employer, then I'd look very much forward to working with you and accompanying you and your colleagues on your discovery journey.

Maybe you were looking for a ready-to-use blueprint to a success-guaranteed working-from-home strategy. Well then, I hope you won't be too disappointed that this is not it. Maybe I should have told you earlier that this has never been *my intention with this book.*

As a coach I am not "telling" people what *I* think *they* should do. As a coach I help my clients find *their best practices*, neither mine nor what other companies think are theirs; as these might not fit at all for *you,* the client I am working with. What I am trying to do here with this book is to **share my model and to provide a tool.**

How *you* put the tool to work for you, that's in your hands.

If you need help, if you have any questions at any time, do reach out! I am always happy to chat and see how I can support you or even work with you.

As stated in the beginning, the PPAS Maturity Model in this book was used to look at changes happening in the workplace due to the move from office workplaces to workplaces at home or anywhere due to a pandemic. However, the PPAS Maturity Model is versatile, and can be adapted to just about *any* change process or change initiative by customizing the discovery questions.

Resources and References

In the sequence of their appearance in the guide

1. Franzen-Waschke, Ute, (2020) *Forbes*: **On the Precipice of A Culture Shift, Adaptation May Come at Warp Speed**.

2. David, Andrew (2016) **The Small Office Home Office Workers Report**

3. Abrams, Zara (2019). **The future of remote work**

4. Kolb's learning cycle

5. Virtual Collaboration.Works

6. The European C-IQ Collective

7. Rigby K., Sutherland J., Takeuchi H. **Embracing Agile** (2016)

8. SAP – company website

9. Microsoft Office 365 – company website

10. Atlassian Products Website

11. The Smart Factory by Deloitte

12. SAP News: SAP and Microsoft Expand Partnership and Integrate Microsoft Teams Across Solutions

13. Slack – company website

14. Trello – company website

15. Mural – company website

16. Miro – company website

17. Ideaclouds – company website

18. Monday.Com – company website

19. Asana – company website

20. Zoom – company website

21. Wonder – company website

22. Howspace – company website

23. Bender, Ruth: **Escape to the Country: Why City Living Is Losing Its Appeal During the Pandemic.** (2020)

24. Scholz, Kai-Alexander (2020): **Are Berlin residents packing up and leaving the city to flee the coronavirus?**

25. Wikipedia on "rural internet"

26. Rothbard, N.P. (2020) **Building Work-Life Boundaries in the WFH Era**.

27. **Coronavirus: Domestic electricity use up during day as nation works from home** (2020)

28. Harvard Business Review - Big Idea: The New Reality of WFH

Please note that any statements made in this guide around use of technology in an organization is based on the experience at the time this guide was written and will have emerged and progressed in the meantime.

About the Author

Ute Franzen-Waschke enjoys working in an international environment and is passionate about developing people—especially when they are challenged with relationships at work, change initiatives, corporate culture, and communication in a work environment that has become more and more complex. Every client is different, and so Ute's approach is custom-tailored to the individual needs of the client and the organization.

When coaching one to one, she helps her clients to build on their natural strengths and to develop confidence in various business situations. And if they are stuck, she is there to help develop new perspectives.

When working with teams or groups in corporate settings an integral part is to facilitate trust building and a healthy communication culture, which is the best fertile ground for anything the team and the organization wants to accomplish.

Ute has worked over the past decades with suppliers to the automotive industry, insurance sector, and consultancies.

She holds an MA in International Business Communication and Coaching (WBIS) and is a Certified Team Coach and Trainer. Ute is certified in Judith E. Glaser's body of work Conversational Intelligence® (C-IQ) and The REACH Method and embodies both frameworks when working with her clients. Ute trains and certifies coaches with Personal Change Systems and Prof. Andy Molinsky, PhD for The REACH Method, and is a member of the Certification and Leadership Team.

Ute has a strong desire to constantly learn and develop and therefore pays particular attention to her personal and professional development. Before becoming self-employed, Ute worked for more than a decade in multinationals as an employee both in her home country as well as abroad. With that comes a very good understanding of the business situations that organizations and corporate clients are facing. Following her work around the PPAS Maturity Model, Ute submitted a research proposal to the University of Chester looking into what makes individuals and companies thrive in a working-from-anywhere era, which was accepted and started in February 2021.

Made in the USA
Coppell, TX
19 November 2021

66037757R00050